Tomato Crops

by Grace Hansen

Abdo Kids Jumbo is an Imprint of Abdo Kids
abdobooks.com

abdobooks.com

Published by Abdo Kids, a division of ABDO, P.O. Box 398166, Minneapolis, Minnesota 55439.
Copyright © 2024 by Abdo Consulting Group, Inc. International copyrights reserved in all countries.
No part of this book may be reproduced in any form without written permission from the publisher.
Abdo Kids Jumbo™ is a trademark and logo of Abdo Kids.

Printed in the United States of America, North Mankato, Minnesota.

052023

092023

 THIS BOOK CONTAINS
RECYCLED MATERIALS

Photo Credits: Alamy, Getty Images, Shutterstock

Production Contributors: Teddy Borth, Jennie Forsberg, Grace Hansen
Design Contributors: Victoria Bates, Candice Keimig

Library of Congress Control Number: 2022946806

Publisher's Cataloging-in-Publication Data

Names: Hansen, Grace, author.

Title: Tomato crops / by Grace Hansen

Description: Minneapolis, Minnesota : Abdo Kids, 2024 | Series: Agriculture in the USA! | Includes online
    resources and index.

Identifiers: ISBN 9781098266226 (lib. bdg.) | ISBN 9781098266929 (ebook) | ISBN 9781098267278
    (Read-to-me ebook)

Subjects: LCSH: Crops--Juvenile literature. | Agriculture--Juvenile literature. | Farming--Juvenile
    literature. | Field crops--Juvenile literature.

Classification: DDC 635.64--dc23

Table of Contents

A Favorite Crop

Tomatoes are one of the most widely consumed vegetable crops. Five countries grow 70% of the world's tomatoes. China grows the most.

United States

Turkey

Egypt

China

India

The History of Tomatoes

The **Aztecs** were the first known people to grow tomatoes. They called the plant *tomatl*, meaning "swelling fruit." This is because tomatoes are a fruit. In cooking, they are considered a vegetable.

The tomato was brought back to Europe during the Spanish **conquest**. The Spanish called the plant *tomate*. By the 16th century, tomatoes had spread throughout the world.

Growing Tomatoes

In the United States, California and Florida grow the most tomatoes. California leads in the **processed** tomato market. Florida is a leader in the fresh market.

California

Florida

Tomato plants love the sun and warm, dry weather.

They are sensitive to frost.

In places that are not warm year round, tomatoes can grow in greenhouses.

Farmers plant tomatoes for **processing** on the ground. These tomatoes are **bred** to ripen on the vine at the same time. This makes for an easier **harvest**.

Fresh tomatoes are grown on **trellises**. They are handpicked. Fresh tomatoes are often picked while they are hard and green. They will continue to ripen.

17

The **harvested** tomatoes are cleaned and kept cool. Fresh tomatoes are delivered to grocery stores.

Processed tomatoes are sent to processing plants. They will be made into tomato paste, sauces, and canned products.

Tomato Growth Stages

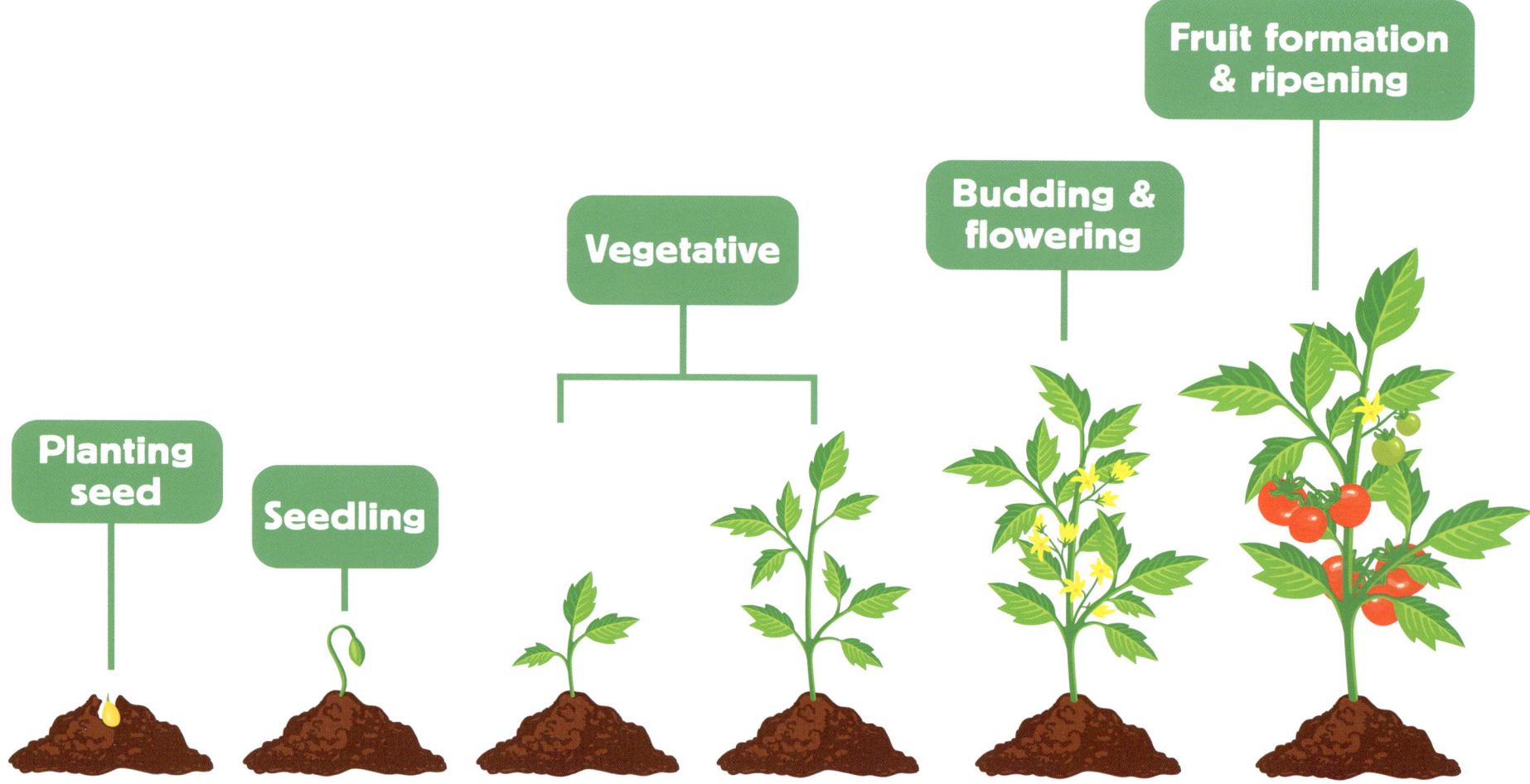

Glossary

Aztec – a member of a Nahuatl-speaking people who in the 15th and early 16th centuries ruled a large empire in what is now central and southern Mexico.

bred – made to act or look a certain way.

conquest – the act or process of conquering.

harvest – the gathering of ripe crops, the crops or the amount of crops gathered, or the season in which they are gathered.

processed – treated or prepared by a particular series of actions.

trellis – a structure often used as a support for climbing plants.

Index

Abdo Kids
ONLINE
FREE! ONLINE MULTIMEDIA RESOURCES

Visit **abdokids.com** to access crafts, games, videos, and more!

Use Abdo Kids code
ATK6226
or scan this QR code!